ALI BABA

FOOLING THE FORTY THIEVES

AN ARABIAN TALE

GRAPHIC UNIVERSE™

STORY BY
MARIE P. CROALL
PENCILS AND INKS BY
CLINT HILINSKI

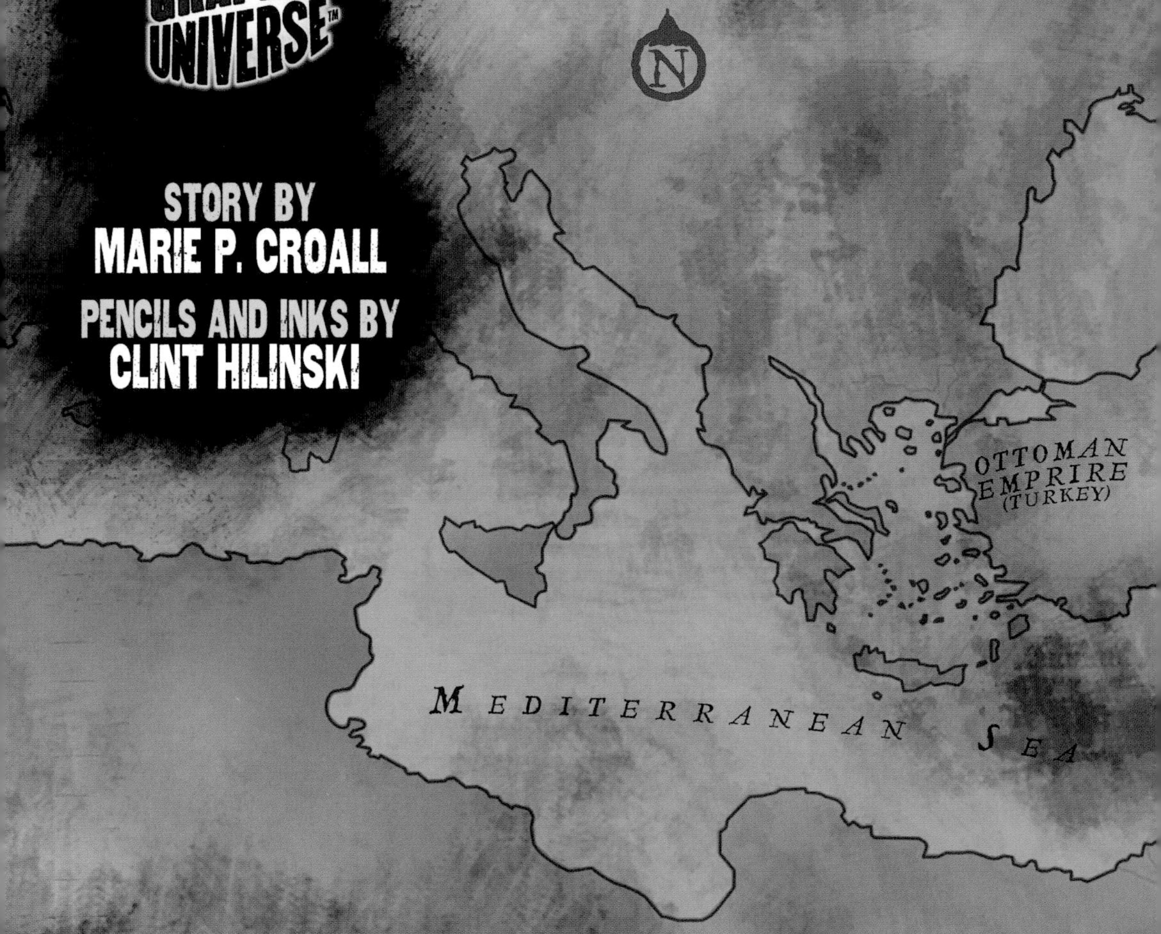
N
OTTOMAN
EMPRIRE
(TURKEY)
MEDITERRANEAN SEA

THIS MAP SHOWS THE LANDS OF THE MIDDLE EAST AS THEY WERE KNOWN AROUND A.D. 1500, WHEN THE STORY OF ALI BABA WAS WRITTEN IN ARABIC.

ALI BABA

FOOLING THE FORTY THIEVES

AN ARABIAN TALE

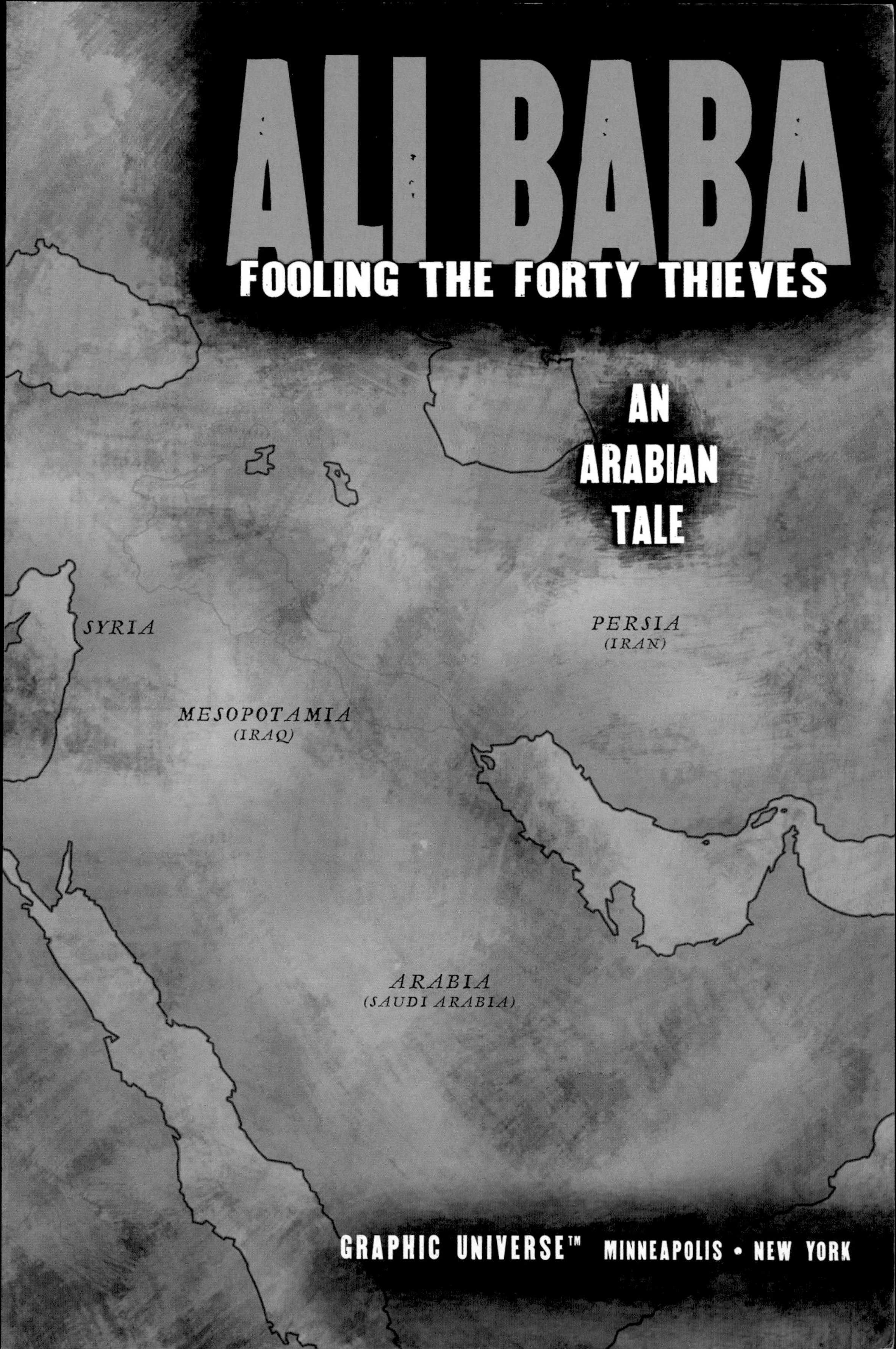
SYRIA
PERSIA
(IRAN)
MESOPOTAMIA
(IRAQ)
ARABIA
(SAUDI ARABIA)

GRAPHIC UNIVERSE™ MINNEAPOLIS • NEW YORK

ALI BABA IS A CHARACTER IN *ARABIAN NIGHTS*. ALSO CALLED *THE THOUSAND AND ONE NIGHTS*, THIS BOOK IS A CLASSIC WORK OF ARABIC LITERATURE. THE WORK IS MADE UP OF APPROXIMATELY TWO HUNDRED STORIES FROM PERSIA, INDIA, AND OTHER COUNTRIES IN AND NEAR THE MIDDLE EAST. ITS STORIES WERE COLLECTED AND WRITTEN DOWN IN ARABIC IN ABOUT A.D. 1500. BRITISH SCHOLARS SIR RICHARD F. BURTON AND JOHN PAYNE TRANSLATED THE STORIES INTO ENGLISH IN THE 1800s.

IN CREATING THE STORY OF ALI BABA, AUTHOR MARIE P. CROALL WORKED FROM *ARABIAN NIGHTS VOLUME I: THE MARVELS AND WONDERS OF THE THOUSAND AND ONE NIGHTS*, ADAPTED FROM RICHARD F. BURTON'S UNEXPURGATED TRANSLATION BY JACK ZIPES. ARTIST CLINT HILINSKI CONSULTED NUMEROUS HISTORICAL RESOURCES TO SHAPE THE VISUAL CONTENT OF THE TALE. IN ADDITION, ALLAN T. KOHL, ART HISTORIAN AND VISUAL RESOURCES LIBRARIAN AT THE MINNEAPOLIS COLLEGE OF ART AND DESIGN, LENT HIS EXPERTISE TO THE PROJECT BY REVIEWING BOTH TEXT AND ART. KOHL HAS STUDIED THE ARABIAN NIGHTS TALES AND AUTHORED AN ARTICLE ON ONE OF THE STORIES IN THE COLLECTION.

STORY BY MARIE P. CROALL

PENCILS AND INKS BY CLINT HILINSKI

COLORING BY HI-FI COLOUR DESIGN

LETTERING BY MARSHALL DILLON AND TERRI DELGADO

CONSULTANT: ALLAN T. KOHL, M.A., MINNEAPOLIS COLLEGE OF ART AND DESIGN

Copyright © 2008 by Lerner Publishing Group, Inc.

Graphic Universe™ is a trademark of Lerner Publishing Group, Inc.

All rights reserved. International copyright secured. No part of this book may be reproduced, stored in a retrieval system, or transmitted in any form or by any means—electronic, mechanical, photocopying, recording, or otherwise—without the prior written permission of Lerner Publishing Group, Inc., except for the inclusion of brief quotations in an acknowledged review.

Graphic Universe™
A division of Lerner Publishing Group, Inc.
241 First Avenue North
Minneapolis, MN 55401 U.S.A.

Website address: www.lernerbooks.com

Library of Congress Cataloging-in-Publication Data

Croall, Marie P.
    Ali Baba: fooling the forty thieves : an Arabian tale : story / by Marie P. Croall ; pencils and inks by Clint Hilinski.
        p.   cm. — (Graphic myths and legends)
    Includes bibliographical references and index.
    ISBN: 978-0-8225-7525-2 (lib. bdg. : alk. paper)
    I. Hilinski, Clint. II. Ali Baba (Folk tale)
III. Arabian nights. IV. Title.
PZ8.C9694A1 2008
398'.352—dc22   2007019741

Manufactured in the United States of America
2 3 4 5 6 7 - DP - 14 13 12 11 10 09

ALI BABA AND THE FOREST ... 7

INSIDE THE CAVE ... 12

KASIM AND HIS WIFE ... 17

MORGIANA AND THE TAILOR ... 27

THE CAPTAIN'S PLAN ... 34

MORGIANA'S DANCE ... 39

GLOSSARY AND PRONUNCIATION GUIDE ... 46

FURTHER READING AND WEBSITES ... 47

CREATING *ALI BABA: FOOLING THE FORTY THIEVES* ... 47

INDEX ... 48

ABOUT THE AUTHOR AND THE ARTIST ... 48

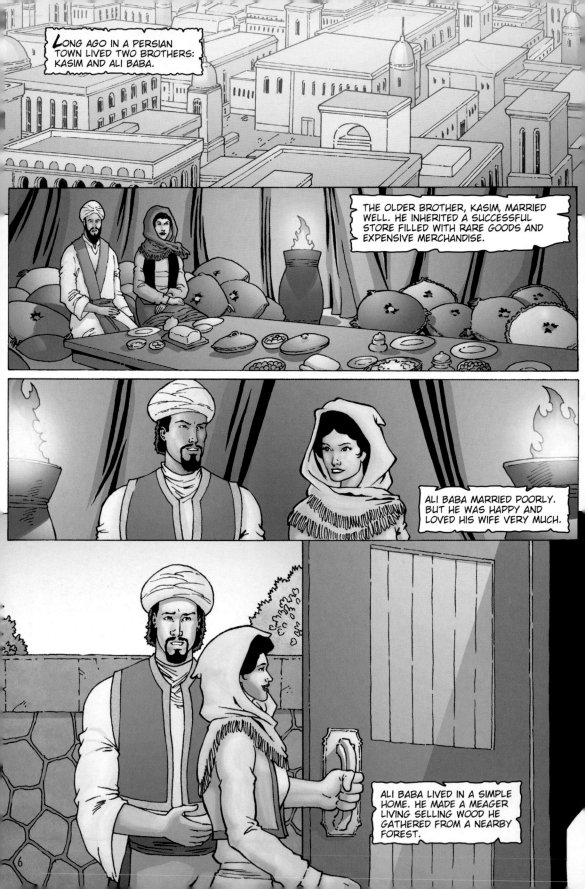

LONG AGO IN A PERSIAN TOWN LIVED TWO BROTHERS: KASIM AND ALI BABA.

THE OLDER BROTHER, KASIM, MARRIED WELL. HE INHERITED A SUCCESSFUL STORE FILLED WITH RARE GOODS AND EXPENSIVE MERCHANDISE.

ALI BABA MARRIED POORLY. BUT HE WAS HAPPY AND LOVED HIS WIFE VERY MUCH.

ALI BABA LIVED IN A SIMPLE HOME. HE MADE A MEAGER LIVING SELLING WOOD HE GATHERED FROM A NEARBY FOREST.

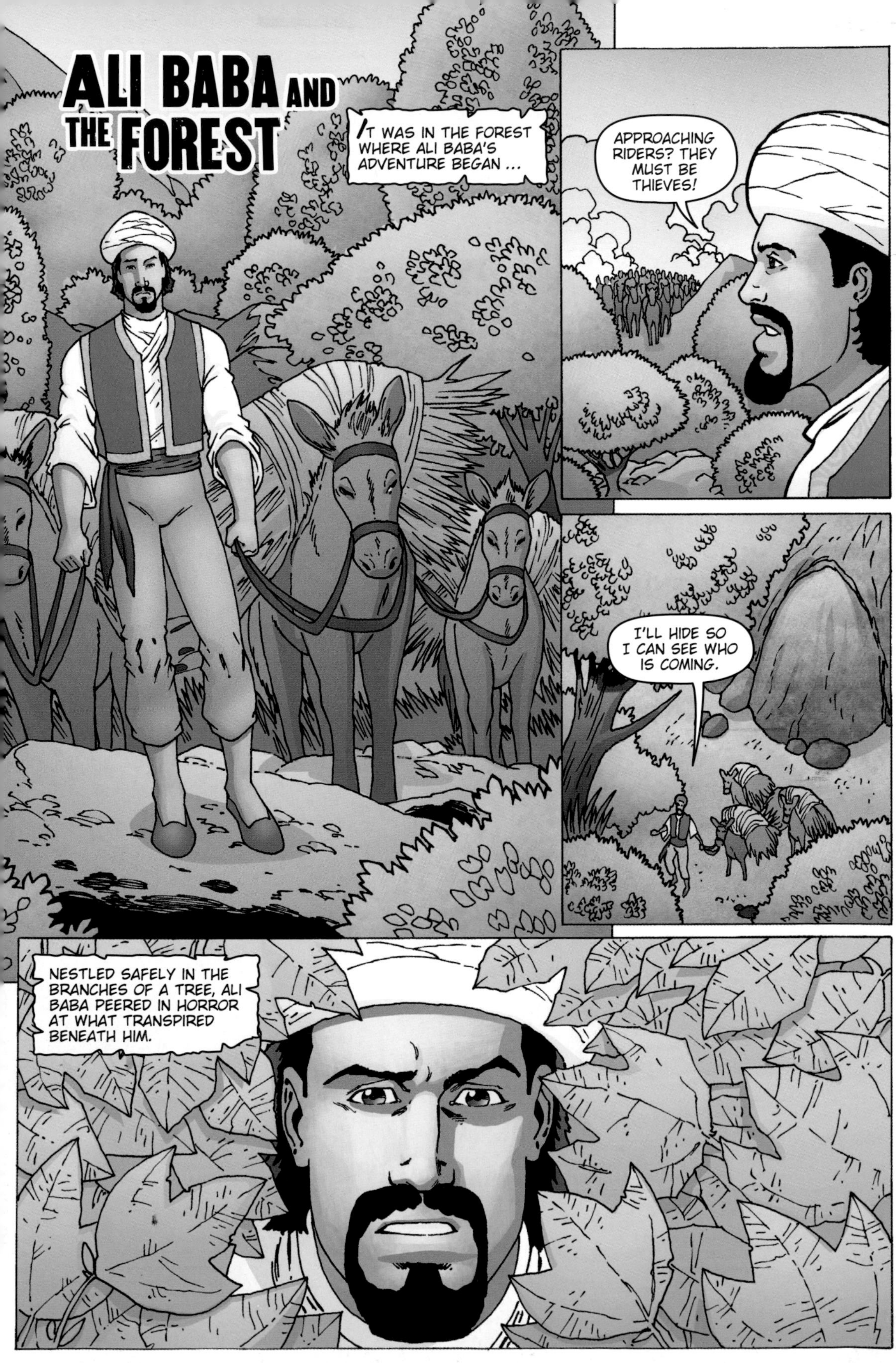
ALI BABA AND THE FOREST
IT WAS IN THE FOREST WHERE ALI BABA'S ADVENTURE BEGAN ...
APPROACHING RIDERS? THEY MUST BE THIEVES!
I'LL HIDE SO I CAN SEE WHO IS COMING.
NESTLED SAFELY IN THE BRANCHES OF A TREE, ALI BABA PEERED IN HORROR AT WHAT TRANSPIRED BENEATH HIM.

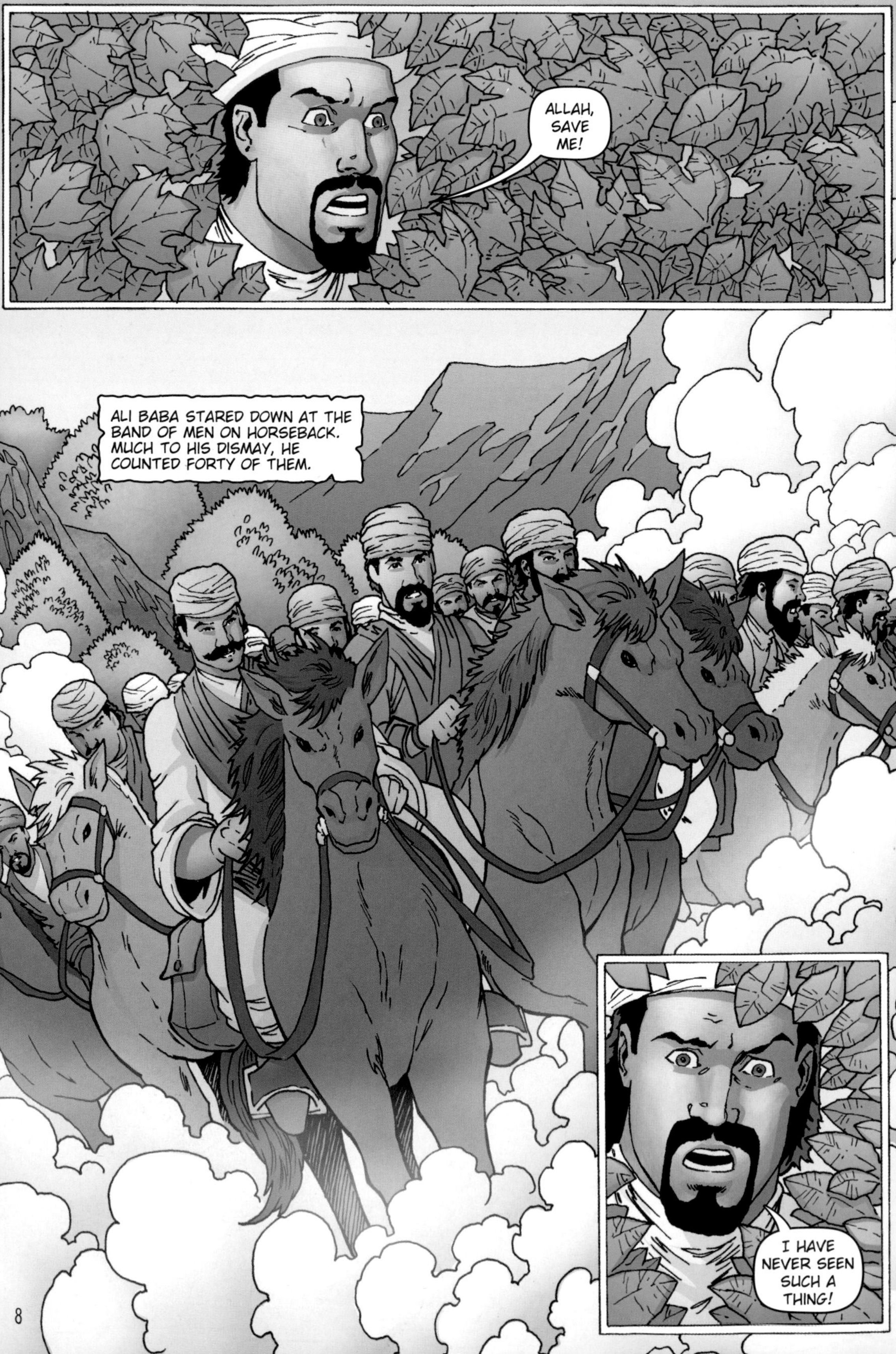
ALLAH, SAVE ME!
ALI BABA STARED DOWN AT THE BAND OF MEN ON HORSEBACK. MUCH TO HIS DISMAY, HE COUNTED FORTY OF THEM.
I HAVE NEVER SEEN SUCH A THING!

THE RIDERS DISMOUNTED THEIR HORSES.

THEY BEGAN REMOVING LARGE SACKS FROM THE ANIMALS.

WHEN THE RIDERS OPENED THE SACKS, ALI BABA COULD SEE THAT THERE WAS A FORTUNE INSIDE.

THEY *ARE* THIEVES.

SUDDENLY THE THIEVES' CAPTAIN EMERGED FROM THE GROUP. HE SHOVED HIS MEN ASIDE AND APPROACHED A NEARBY ROCK ...

AND THEN HE SPOKE SOME VERY STRANGE WORDS.

OPEN SESAME!

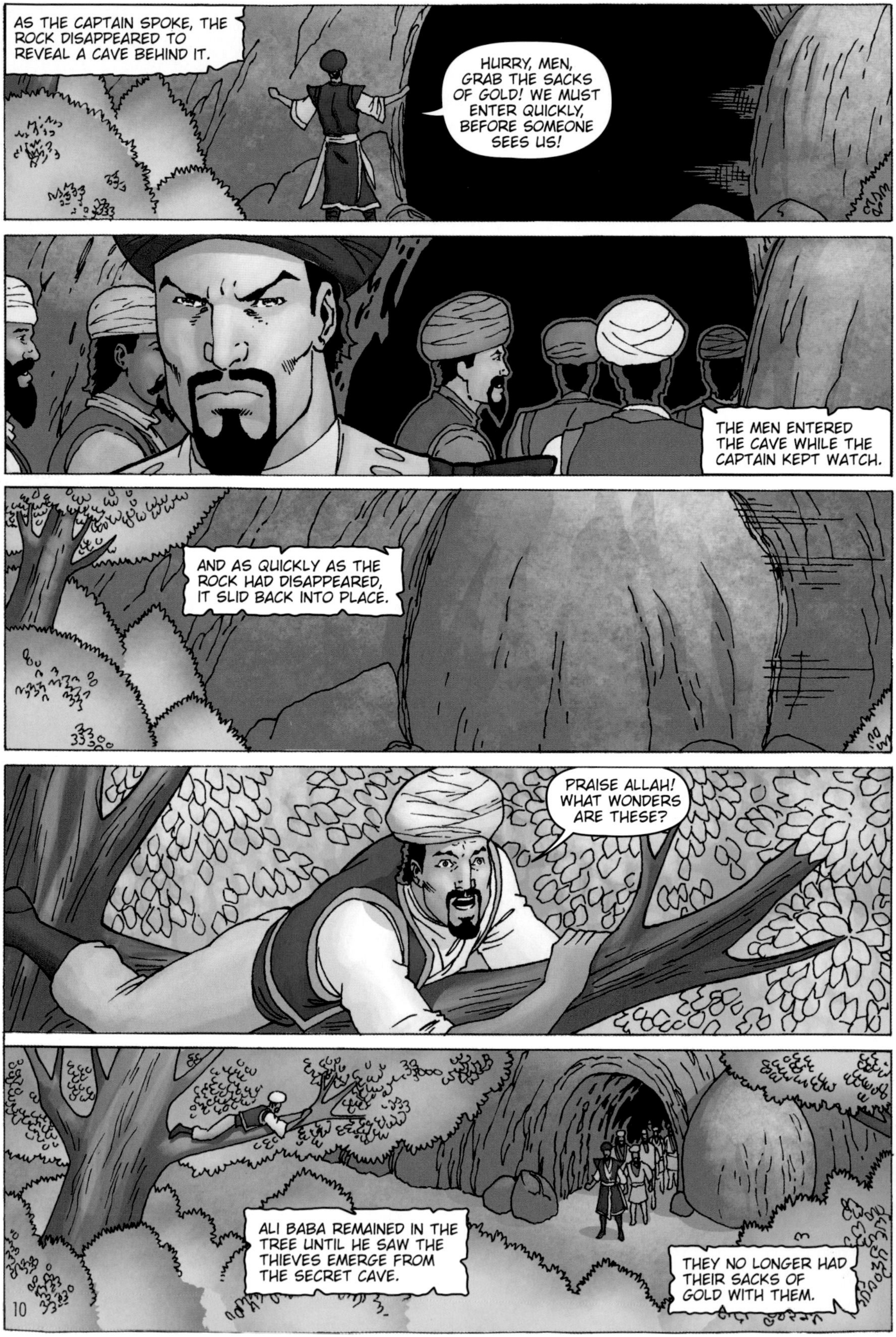
AS THE CAPTAIN SPOKE, THE ROCK DISAPPEARED TO REVEAL A CAVE BEHIND IT.
HURRY, MEN, GRAB THE SACKS OF GOLD! WE MUST ENTER QUICKLY, BEFORE SOMEONE SEES US!
THE MEN ENTERED THE CAVE WHILE THE CAPTAIN KEPT WATCH.
AND AS QUICKLY AS THE ROCK HAD DISAPPEARED, IT SLID BACK INTO PLACE.
PRAISE ALLAH! WHAT WONDERS ARE THESE?
ALI BABA REMAINED IN THE TREE UNTIL HE SAW THE THIEVES EMERGE FROM THE SECRET CAVE.
THEY NO LONGER HAD THEIR SACKS OF GOLD WITH THEM.

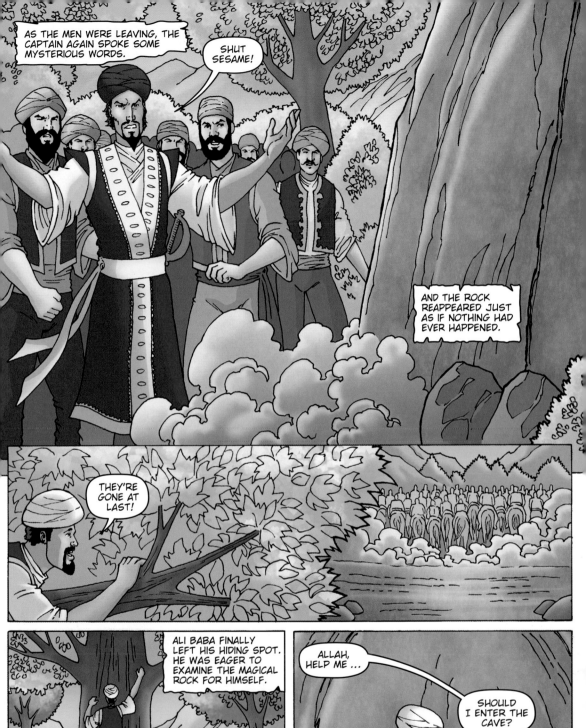

AS THE MEN WERE LEAVING, THE CAPTAIN AGAIN SPOKE SOME MYSTERIOUS WORDS.

SHUT SESAME!

AND THE ROCK REAPPEARED JUST AS IF NOTHING HAD EVER HAPPENED.

THEY'RE GONE AT LAST!

ALI BABA FINALLY LEFT HIS HIDING SPOT. HE WAS EAGER TO EXAMINE THE MAGICAL ROCK FOR HIMSELF.

ALLAH, HELP ME ...

SHOULD I ENTER THE CAVE?

INSIDE THE CAVE

*F*EARFULLY, ALI BABA SPOKE THE WORDS HE'D HEARD THE CAPTAIN SAY.

OPEN SESAME?

HE LOOKED ON IN WONDER AS THE ROCK DISAPPEARED.

PRAISE ALLAH, I'LL ALWAYS REMEMBER THOSE MAGIC WORDS!

WHAT ALI BABA SAW IN THE CAVE WAS MORE WONDROUS THAN ANYTHING HE COULD HAVE IMAGINED.

SUCH RICHES! THEY MUST HAVE BEEN HIDING THINGS HERE FOR GENERATIONS.

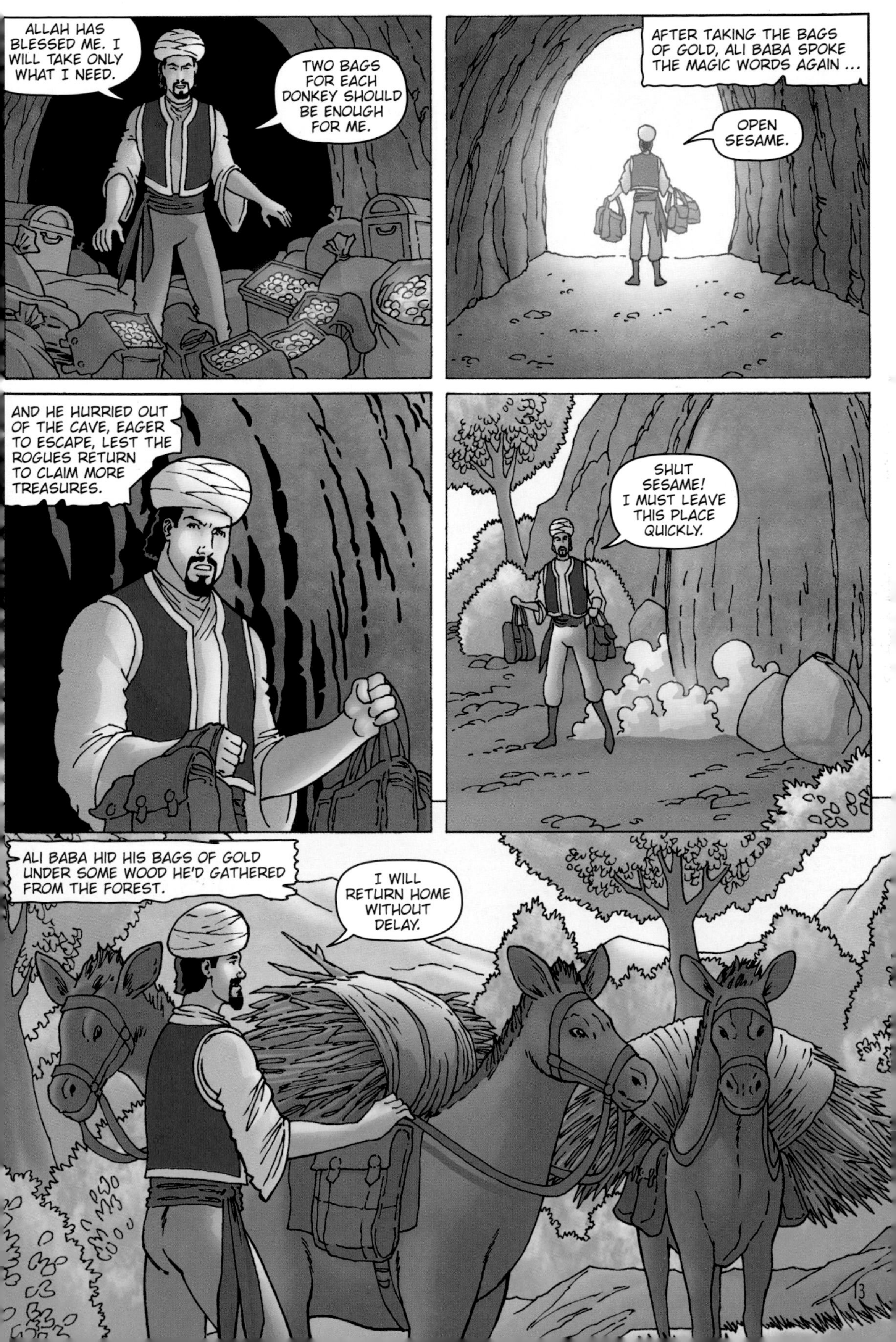
ALLAH HAS BLESSED ME. I WILL TAKE ONLY WHAT I NEED.
TWO BAGS FOR EACH DONKEY SHOULD BE ENOUGH FOR ME.
AFTER TAKING THE BAGS OF GOLD, ALI BABA SPOKE THE MAGIC WORDS AGAIN ...
OPEN SESAME.
AND HE HURRIED OUT OF THE CAVE, EAGER TO ESCAPE, LEST THE ROGUES RETURN TO CLAIM MORE TREASURES.
SHUT SESAME! I MUST LEAVE THIS PLACE QUICKLY.
ALI BABA HID HIS BAGS OF GOLD UNDER SOME WOOD HE'D GATHERED FROM THE FOREST.
I WILL RETURN HOME WITHOUT DELAY.

A SHORT TIME LATER, ALI BABA RODE INTO HIS VILLAGE. HE HOPED NO ONE WOULD NOTICE THE BAGS HIS DONKEYS WERE CARRYING.

HOME AT LAST!

I CAN'T WAIT TO SHOW THIS FORTUNE TO MY DEAR WIFE.

WHEN ALI BABA ENTERED HIS HOME, HE FOUND HIS WIFE PREPARING A MEAL.

HUSBAND, ARE YOU WELL?

SHHHH. LOOK AT THIS.

YOU THIEF! WHERE DID YOU GET ALL THIS GOLD?

WHOM DID YOU STEAL IT FROM?

ALI BABA HAD TO SPEAK QUICKLY TO CALM HER FEARS.

DO NOT WORRY, MY DEAR WIFE. I AM NO ROBBER. REJOICE IN OUR GOOD FORTUNE!

LISTEN, AND I WILL TELL YOU THE STORY.

AFTER ALI BABA HAD EMPTIED THE BAGS OF GOLD, HE TOLD HIS WIFE THE TALE OF THE THIEVES AND THE CAVE.

... AND AFTER I TOOK THE GOLD, I HURRIED BACK HOME BEFORE ANYONE COULD SEE ME.

PRAISE ALLAH! LET US COUNT OUR FORTUNE.

15

WE HAVE NO TIME TO COUNT OUR MONEY.

WE MUST BURY IT BEFORE SOMEONE DISCOVERS US.

YOU ARE RIGHT.

BUT ...

LET ME WEIGH THE GOLD. THEN WE WILL HAVE SOME IDEA OF ITS WORTH.

IF YOU MUST— BUT TELL NO ONE! WE CANNOT AFFORD TO RISK REVEALING OUR SECRET!

ALI BABA'S WIFE HURRIED TO KASIM'S HOUSE TO ASK HER SISTER-IN-LAW FOR A SCALE.

NOK NOK NOK

KASIM AND HIS WIFE

SISTER-IN-LAW! LEND ME YOUR SCALES FOR A MOMENT.

DO YOU NEED THE BIGGER OR SMALLER SCALES?

OF COURSE. WAIT HERE.

SMALLER, IF YOU HAVE THEM.

ALI BABA SHOULDN'T HAVE ENOUGH OF ANYTHING TO MEASURE ...

I'LL PUT SOME SUET ON THE BOTTOM OF THE SCALE.

WHATEVER THEY ARE MEASURING WILL STICK TO THE BOTTOM. THEN I'LL KNOW WHAT ALI BABA AND HIS WIFE ARE UP TO.

HERE, SISTER-IN-LAW.

I'LL RETURN YOUR SCALE SOON.

OH, NO HURRY.

ALI BABA'S WIFE MEASURED THE GOLD. MEANWHILE, ALI BABA DUG A HOLE IN THE BACKYARD TO BURY THE TREASURE.

SHORTLY AFTER ALI BABA BURIED THE GOLD, HIS WIFE TOOK THE SCALE BACK TO KASIM'S HOUSE. SHE FELT CERTAIN THAT THE SECRET OF THE GOLD WAS SAFE.

BUT KASIM'S WIFE SOON DISCOVERED THE SECRET. SHE COULD SEE THAT ALI BABA AND HIS WIFE HAD BEEN MEASURING GOLD.

GOLD! I THOUGHT ALI BABA WAS A PAUPER. THIS WHOLE TIME HE'S BEEN HIDING HIS WEALTH FROM US!

WHEN KASIM ARRIVED HOME THAT EVENING, HIS WIFE CONFRONTED HIM WITH THE NEWS OF ALI BABA'S RICHES.

KASIM, YOUR BROTHER HAS BEEN LYING TO YOU.

WHAT ARE YOU SAYING, WIFE?

ALI BABA HAS ONLY BEEN PRETENDING TO BE POOR.

HE HAD EVERYONE FOOLED. HIS WIFE HAD TO BORROW A SCALE TO WEIGH HIS GOLD! HE MUST BE RICH.

HOW DARE HE HIDE HIS WEALTH FROM ME!

GO TO HIM, DEAR HUSBAND. GET HIM TO TELL YOU WHERE HE GOT HIS MONEY.

YES, WIFE, I'LL GO TO HIM FIRST THING IN THE MORNING AND MAKE HIM TELL ME.

THE NEXT MORNING, KASIM ARRIVED AT HIS BROTHER'S HOUSE. HE WASTED NO TIME IN CONFRONTING HIM.

YOU HAVE BEEN HOLDING BACK YOUR RICHES FROM ME!

WHAT DO YOU MEAN?

DON'T THINK YOU CAN FOOL ME! YOU MUST HAVE THOUSANDS OF THESE IF YOU NEED TO WEIGH THEM.

MY WIFE FOUND THIS ONE STUCK TO THE BOTTOM OF THE SCALE.

IF YOU DO NOT TELL ME WHERE YOU GOT THIS GOLD, I'LL TELL THE AUTHORITIES YOU ARE A THIEF. YOU'LL GO TO JAIL!

ALL RIGHT, BROTHER. I'LL TELL YOU EVERYTHING.

THE NEXT DAY, KASIM WENT TO FIND THE PLACE WHERE ALI BABA HAD DISCOVERED THE RICHES. HE WANTED TO GET SOME PRECIOUS COINS FOR HIMSELF.

IF THERE IS AS MUCH GOLD AS ALI BABA SAYS, SOON I WILL BE THE RICHEST MAN IN ALL OF PERSIA.

HE TRIED USING THE PASSWORD HIS BROTHER HAD GIVEN HIM.

THE PASSWORD WORKED!

PRAISE ALLAH.

THIS IS EVEN MORE GOLD THAN I HAD IMAGINED. I WILL BE RICHER THAN ALI BABA!

WITH BAGS OF RICHES FILLED TO THE BRIM, KASIM ATTEMPTED TO EXIT THE CAVE.

OPEN BARLEY!

BUT HE'D FORGOTTEN THE MAGICAL WORDS. KASIM BEGAN TO PANIC. HE FEARED THE THIEVES WOULD SOON RETURN.

ALLAH, SAVE ME ...

OPEN WHEAT! OPEN CORN!? OPEN OATS!?!

OUTSIDE THE CAVE, THE THIEVES WERE FAST APPROACHING.

RRRMMMBBBLL

KASIM COULD HEAR THEM COMING. FRANTICALLY, HE THOUGHT ABOUT WHAT TO DO NEXT.

RRMMBBLL

WHEN THE CAVE DOOR OPENED, KASIM DECIDED TO RUN.

THIS IS MY CHANCE!

IN HIS HURRY TO ESCAPE, KASIM NEARLY COLLIDED WITH THE CAPTAIN.

THE CAPTAIN WAS FURIOUS. HE SHOVED KASIM TO THE GROUND.

THEN ONE OF THE THIEVES USED HIS SHARPENED SCIMITAR TO CUT THE UNFORTUNATE TRESPASSER IN HALF.

SSSHHK

MEN, WE CAN'T AFFORD TO HAVE ANY MORE TRESPASSERS.

CUT THIS INTRUDER'S BODY INTO FOUR PIECES. WE'LL HANG THE PIECES BY THE CAVE'S ENTRANCE. THAT WILL WARN OTHERS WHAT HAPPENS TO THOSE WHO DARE ENTER OUR SECRET HIDING PLACE!

IF THERE ARE ANY MORE INTRUDERS ...

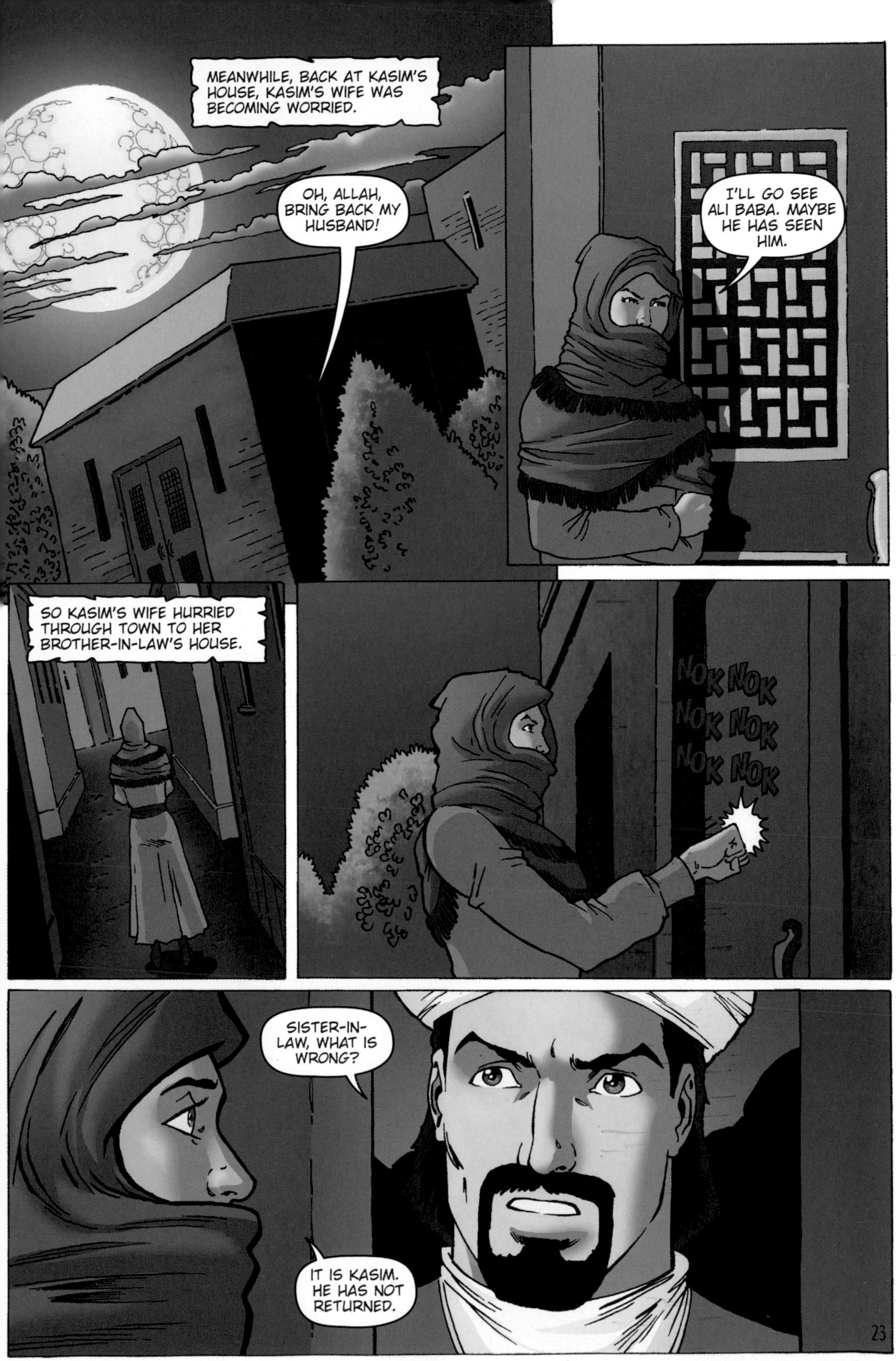

MEANWHILE, BACK AT KASIM'S HOUSE, KASIM'S WIFE WAS BECOMING WORRIED.
OH, ALLAH, BRING BACK MY HUSBAND!
I'LL GO SEE ALI BABA. MAYBE HE HAS SEEN HIM.
SO KASIM'S WIFE HURRIED THROUGH TOWN TO HER BROTHER-IN-LAW'S HOUSE.
NOK NOK NOK NOK NOK NOK
SISTER-IN-LAW, WHAT IS WRONG?
IT IS KASIM. HE HAS NOT RETURNED.

TELL ME WHAT HAS HAPPENED.

HE WENT TO THAT CURSED CAVE. THIS IS ALL MY FAULT.

DO NOT WORRY, SISTER-IN-LAW. I AM SURE HE WAS ONLY DELAYED.

GO HOME AND WAIT FOR HIM. HE WILL RETURN WITH THE SUN.

KASIM'S WIFE WENT HOME, BUT SHE WAS TOO WORRIED TO SLEEP.

WHY DID I MAKE HIM JEALOUS OF ALI BABA?

THIS HAS BECOME A DISASTER.

THE NEXT MORNING, KASIM'S WIFE DECIDED TO RETURN TO ALI BABA'S HOUSE.

ALI BABA IS WISE. HE WILL KNOW WHAT TO DO.

BROTHER-IN-LAW!

BROTHER-IN-LAW!

NOK NOK NOK NOK

THE SUN IS CLIMBING HIGHER IN THE SKY, AND STILL MY HUSBAND HAS NOT RETURNED.

YOU MUST GO TO THAT CAVE AND SEARCH FOR KASIM!

I FEAR TRAGEDY HAS BEFALLEN HIM.

KEEP CALM, SISTER-IN-LAW.

I WILL FIND YOUR HUSBAND.

ALI BABA SET OUT FOR THE CAVE, BUT HE FEARED THE WORST HAD HAPPENED.

KASIM MAY BE IN DANGER. I MUST ENTER QUICKLY.

OPEN SESAME!

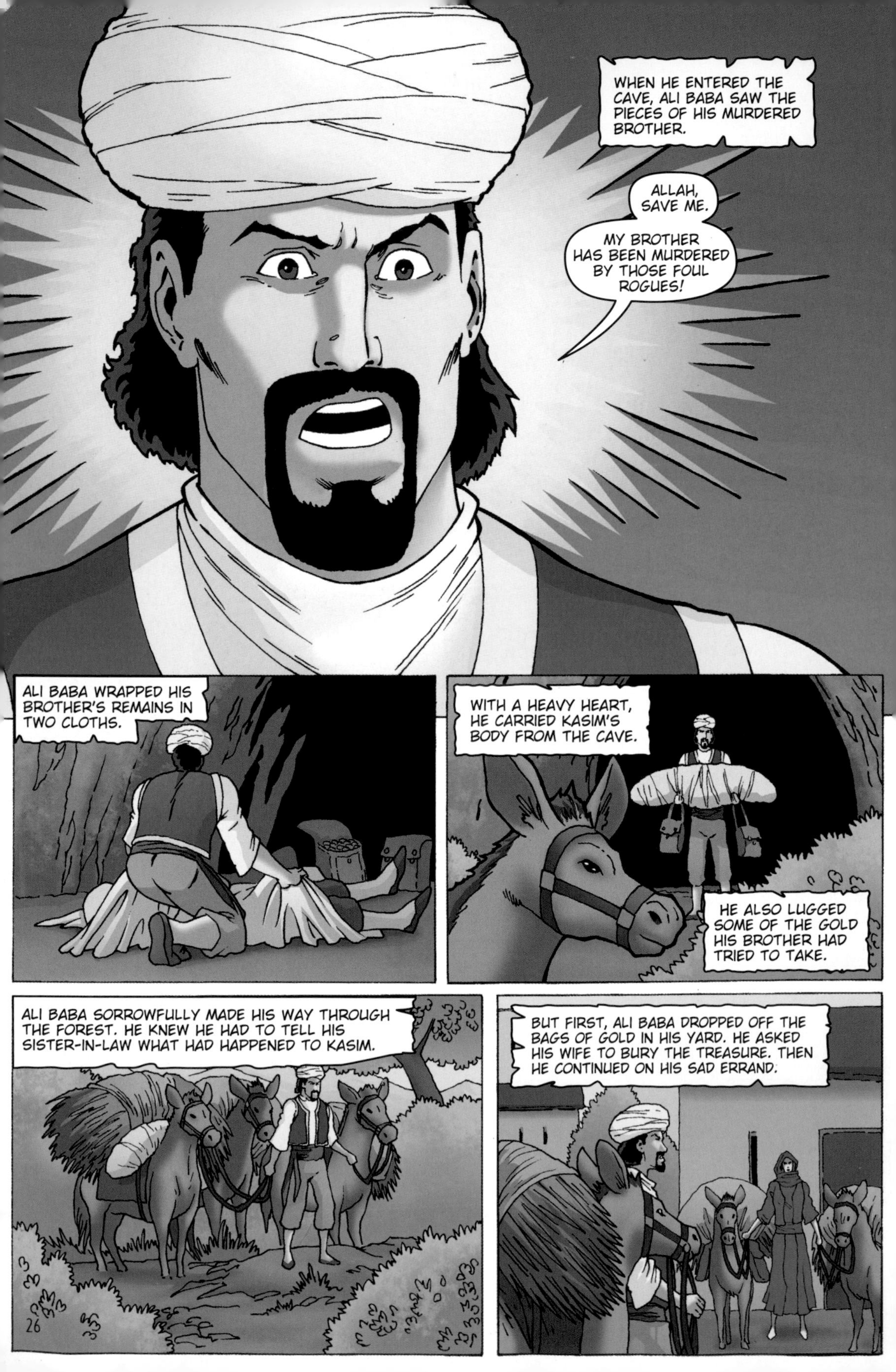
WHEN HE ENTERED THE CAVE, ALI BABA SAW THE PIECES OF HIS MURDERED BROTHER.
ALLAH, SAVE ME.
MY BROTHER HAS BEEN MURDERED BY THOSE FOUL ROGUES!
ALI BABA WRAPPED HIS BROTHER'S REMAINS IN TWO CLOTHS.
WITH A HEAVY HEART, HE CARRIED KASIM'S BODY FROM THE CAVE.
HE ALSO LUGGED SOME OF THE GOLD HIS BROTHER HAD TRIED TO TAKE.
ALI BABA SORROWFULLY MADE HIS WAY THROUGH THE FOREST. HE KNEW HE HAD TO TELL HIS SISTER-IN-LAW WHAT HAD HAPPENED TO KASIM.
BUT FIRST, ALI BABA DROPPED OFF THE BAGS OF GOLD IN HIS YARD. HE ASKED HIS WIFE TO BURY THE TREASURE. THEN HE CONTINUED ON HIS SAD ERRAND.

MORGIANA AND THE TAILOR

ALI BABA SOON ARRIVED AT THE HOME OF HIS SISTER-IN-LAW.

KASIM'S SERVANT, MORGIANA, ANSWERED THE DOOR.

HAS SOME KIND OF HARM BEFALLEN MY MASTER? YOU DO NOT BRING GOOD NEWS.

ENTER QUICKLY.

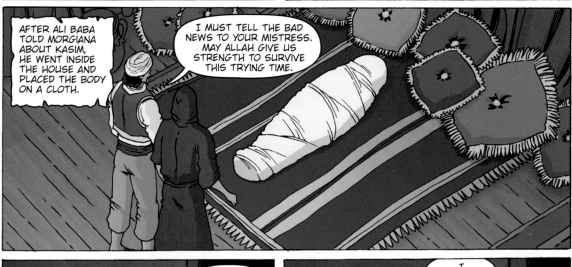

AFTER ALI BABA TOLD MORGIANA ABOUT KASIM, HE WENT INSIDE THE HOUSE AND PLACED THE BODY ON A CLOTH.

I MUST TELL THE BAD NEWS TO YOUR MISTRESS. MAY ALLAH GIVE US STRENGTH TO SURVIVE THIS TRYING TIME.

WHEN ALI BABA TOLD KASIM'S WIFE WHAT HAD HAPPENED, SHE WAS DISTRAUGHT.

WE CANNOT CHANGE WHAT HAS HAPPENED.

BUT WE MUST KEEP THIS SECRET. OUR LIVES DEPEND ON IT.

I UNDERSTAND. I WILL TELL NO ONE.

WHEN YOUR MOURNING IS OVER, MY WIFE AND I WILL JOIN YOU IN YOUR HOME. WE WILL LIVE WITH ONE ANOTHER AS A FAMILY.

MY WIFE WILL BE KIND TO YOU, FOR SHE IS SWEET AND GENTLE.

I AM GRATEFUL TO YOU, FOR EVERYTHING.

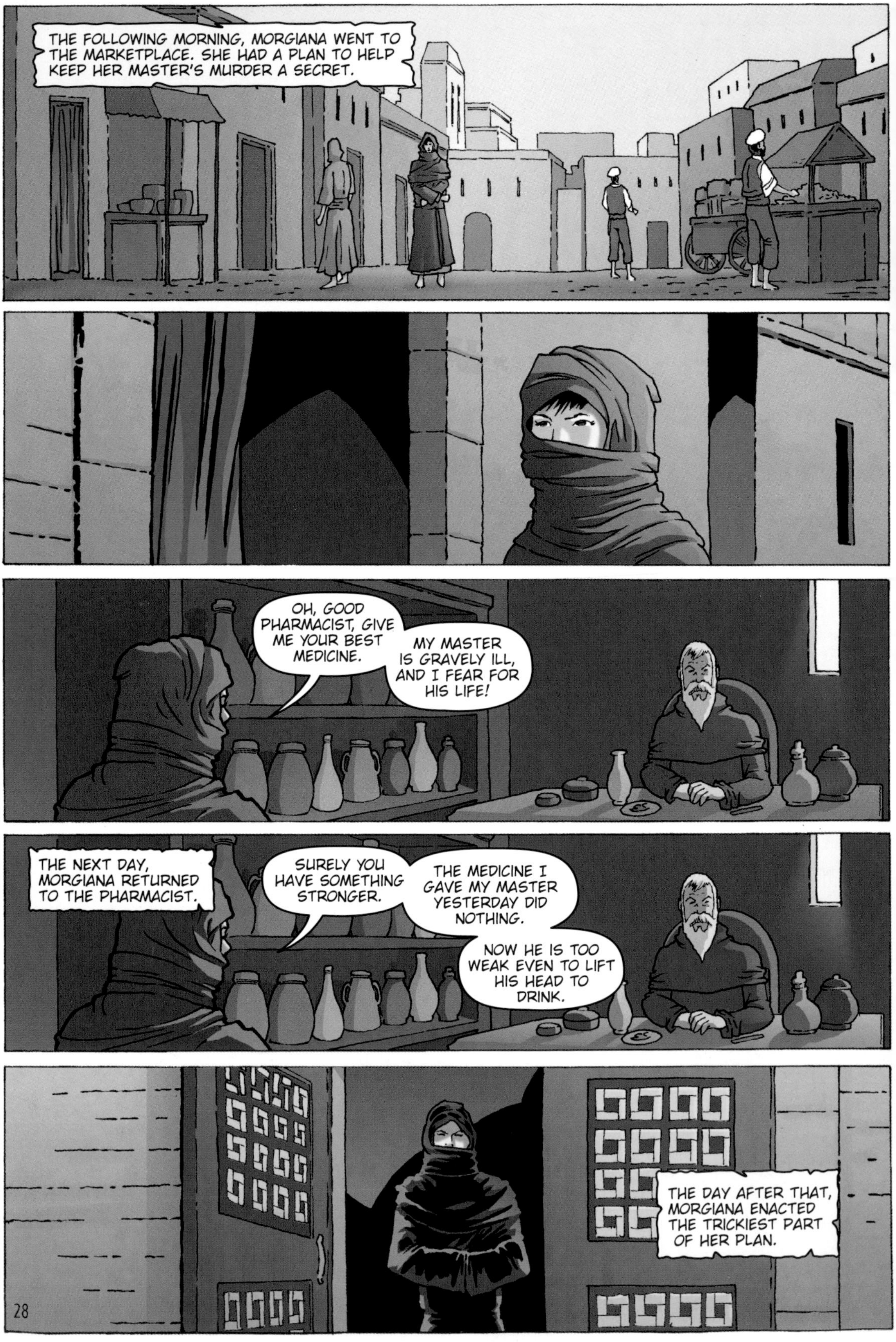
THE FOLLOWING MORNING, MORGIANA WENT TO THE MARKETPLACE. SHE HAD A PLAN TO HELP KEEP HER MASTER'S MURDER A SECRET.
OH, GOOD PHARMACIST, GIVE ME YOUR BEST MEDICINE.
MY MASTER IS GRAVELY ILL, AND I FEAR FOR HIS LIFE!
THE NEXT DAY, MORGIANA RETURNED TO THE PHARMACIST.
SURELY YOU HAVE SOMETHING STRONGER.
THE MEDICINE I GAVE MY MASTER YESTERDAY DID NOTHING.
NOW HE IS TOO WEAK EVEN TO LIFT HIS HEAD TO DRINK.
THE DAY AFTER THAT, MORGIANA ENACTED THE TRICKIEST PART OF HER PLAN.

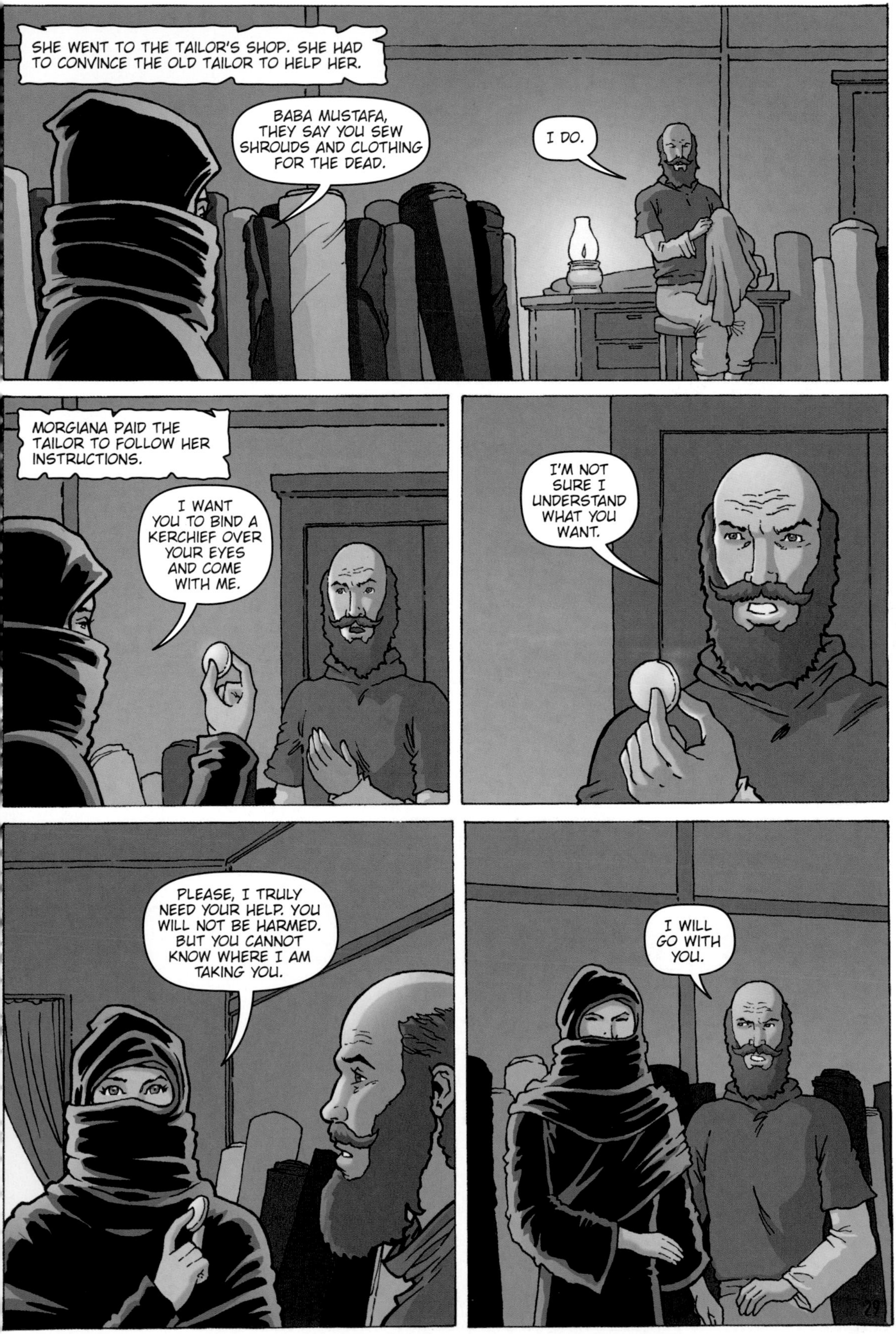
SHE WENT TO THE TAILOR'S SHOP. SHE HAD TO CONVINCE THE OLD TAILOR TO HELP HER.
BABA MUSTAFA, THEY SAY YOU SEW SHROUDS AND CLOTHING FOR THE DEAD.
I DO.
MORGIANA PAID THE TAILOR TO FOLLOW HER INSTRUCTIONS.
I WANT YOU TO BIND A KERCHIEF OVER YOUR EYES AND COME WITH ME.
I'M NOT SURE I UNDERSTAND WHAT YOU WANT.
PLEASE, I TRULY NEED YOUR HELP. YOU WILL NOT BE HARMED. BUT YOU CANNOT KNOW WHERE I AM TAKING YOU.
I WILL GO WITH YOU.
29

MORGIANA LED THE TAILOR TO KASIM'S HOME, WHERE THEY HAD PLACED HIS BODY.

I NEED YOU TO SEW A BODY BACK TOGETHER AND MAKE A SHROUD FOR BURIAL. YOU CAN REMOVE YOUR BLINDFOLD WHILE YOU WORK.

BABA MUSTAFA QUICKLY SET ABOUT PREPARING THE BODY.

WITH KASIM'S BODY IN ONE PIECE, ALI BABA GAVE HIS BROTHER A PROPER FUNERAL.

AS WAS THE CUSTOM, ALI BABA MOVED INTO KASIM'S HOUSE.

KASIM'S SON TOOK OVER THE STORE KASIM HAD OWNED. LIFE SOON RETURNED TO NORMAL.

BUT ALI BABA'S TROUBLES WERE JUST BEGINNING.

BACK AT THE CAVE, THE THIEVES HAD DISCOVERED A SURPRISING SIGHT. THE BODY THEY'D HUNG THERE AS A WARNING HAD DISAPPEARED! SO HAD SOME OF THEIR BAGS OF GOLD.

SOMEONE ELSE KNOWS ABOUT OUR CAVE.

WE MUST FIND OUT WHO THE INTRUDER IS.

MY CAPTAIN, I WILL GO TO THE NEAREST VILLAGE AND SEE WHAT INFORMATION I CAN FIND.

GO EARLY IN THE MORNING, AND REPORT BACK AS SOON AS POSSIBLE.

AT DAWN THE NEXT MORNING, THE THIEF HEADED TO THE TOWN WHERE ALI BABA LIVED TO FIND INFORMATION.

I'LL SEE IF THIS MERCHANT KNOWS ANYTHING.

THE MERCHANT WAS NONE OTHER THAN BABA MUSTAFA, THE TAILOR.

IT'S SO DARK IN YOUR SHOP. HOW DO YOU SEE TO WORK?

THIS IS *NOTHING*. I RECENTLY PREPARED A BODY FOR BURIAL IN A HOME MUCH DARKER THAN THIS.

I WILL GIVE YOU A GOLD PIECE IF YOU CAN SHOW ME WHERE THAT HOME IS.

ALAS, I CANNOT. I WAS BLINDFOLDED.

I COULD BLINDFOLD YOU, AND THEN WE CAN RETRACE YOUR STEPS.

IF YOU WISH.

IS THIS THE PLACE?

THIS IS THE ONE.

THERE. THIS WHITE X WILL HELP US FIND THE HOUSE AGAIN.

BUT MORGIANA SAW THE CHALK MARK.

SHE IMMEDIATELY BECAME SUSPICIOUS.

WHOEVER MADE THIS MARK IS UP TO NO GOOD. PERHAPS HE INTENDS TO HARM ALI BABA. I MUST DO SOMETHING ...

NO ONE WILL FIND ALI BABA'S HOUSE NOW!

WHEN THE CAPTAIN WENT TO FIND THE TRESPASSER, HE WAS IN FOR A SURPRISE.

HE FAILED ME! HE SAID THE RIGHT HOUSE HAD AN X ON THE DOOR. BUT *ALL* THESE DOORS ARE MARKED!

BACK IN THE CAVE, THE CAPTAIN SENT ANOTHER MAN TO FIND ALI BABA.

THE FIRST THIEF FAILED ME AND HAS BEEN TAKEN AWAY.

WHICH OF YOU WILL NOT FAIL ME?

I WILL NOT. SEND ME!

THE SECOND THIEF WENT TO KASIM'S HOUSE JUST AS THE FIRST THIEF HAD.

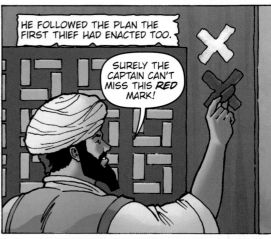

HE FOLLOWED THE PLAN THE FIRST THIEF HAD ENACTED TOO.

SURELY THE CAPTAIN CAN'T MISS THIS *RED* MARK!

BUT HE DIDN'T COUNT ON THE CLEVERNESS OF MORGIANA.

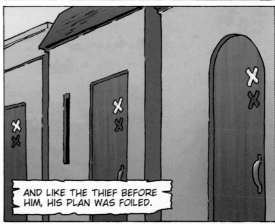

AND LIKE THE THIEF BEFORE HIM, HIS PLAN WAS FOILED.

THEY HAVE FAILED ME TOO MANY TIMES!

I WILL GO TO THE HOUSE MYSELF AND MEMORIZE THE LOCATION.

THE CAPTAIN'S PLAN

WHEN THE CAPTAIN RETURNED THAT EVENING, HE FELT QUITE SATISFIED.

I HAVE DONE WHAT THE OTHER TWO COULD NOT. I FOLLOWED THE TAILOR, BUT INSTEAD OF MARKING THE DOORS ...

I MEMORIZED THE LOCATION. I WILL BE ABLE TO FIND IT AGAIN!

NOW, HERE IS THE PLAN.

THE NEXT DAY, THE CAPTAIN RETURNED TO THE VILLAGE WITH HIS MEN, WHO WERE HIDDEN IN LARGE OIL POTS.

THE CAPTAIN FOUND ALI BABA'S HOUSE.

GOOD SIR, I AM A LOWLY OIL MERCHANT, TRAVELING FAR FROM HOME.

I HAVE ARRIVED TOO LATE TO GET LODGING, AND I NEED A PLACE TO STORE MY DONKEYS AND OIL POTS FOR THE NIGHT.

FRIEND, YOU CAN STAY WITH ME. YOU CAN KEEP YOUR DONKEYS AND OIL POTS IN MY YARD. I'LL HAVE ABDULLAH, MY SERVING BOY, LOOK AFTER THEM.

ABDULLAH, OUR GUEST IS AN OIL MERCHANT. HIS POTS ARE IN BACK WITH HIS DONKEYS.

SEE THAT THEY ARE WELL TAKEN CARE OF. MORGIANA, PREPARE A FEAST FOR OUR TIRED FRIEND.

WE WILL SHOW HIM THE HOSPITALITY BEFITTING AN HONORED GUEST.

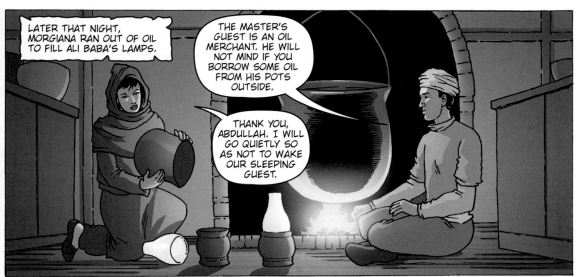

LATER THAT NIGHT, MORGIANA RAN OUT OF OIL TO FILL ALI BABA'S LAMPS.

THE MASTER'S GUEST IS AN OIL MERCHANT. HE WILL NOT MIND IF YOU BORROW SOME OIL FROM HIS POTS OUTSIDE.

THANK YOU, ABDULLAH. I WILL GO QUIETLY SO AS NOT TO WAKE OUR SLEEPING GUEST.

I WILL TAKE ONLY WHAT I NEED.

AS MORGIANA NEARED ONE OF THE POTS, SHE HEARD A VOICE.

IS IT TIME TO STRIKE?

MORGIANA KNEW THAT SOMETHING WASN'T RIGHT. SHE CUPPED HER HANDS OVER HER MOUTH AND DISGUISED HER VOICE. SPEAKING IN LOW AND MUFFLED TONES, SHE DID HER BEST IMPRESSION OF HER MASTER'S GUEST.

NOT YET.

THEN, SUDDENLY, MORGIANA KNEW EXACTLY WHAT WAS GOING ON. IN SHOCK, SHE WHISPERED TO HERSELF.

ALLAH, SAVE US! THE MAN SLEEPING INSIDE IS NO MERCHANT. AND THESE POTS DO NOT CONTAIN OIL. OUR GUEST MUST BE THE CAPTAIN OF THE THIEVES.

HIS MEN ARE LYING IN WAIT TO KILL US!

35

MORGIANA MOVED ON TO THE NEXT POT, CONTINUING TO DISGUISE HER VOICE ...

IS IT TIME?

NOT YET.

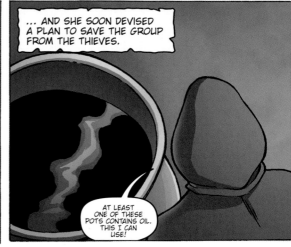

... AND SHE SOON DEVISED A PLAN TO SAVE THE GROUP FROM THE THIEVES.

AT LEAST ONE OF THESE POTS CONTAINS OIL. THIS I CAN USE!

WHEN MORGIANA RETURNED TO THE HOUSE, SHE PUT HER PLAN INTO ACTION.

SHE BOILED A LARGE VAT OF OIL FROM THE POT OUTSIDE.

THEN SHE PROCEEDED TO DUMP THE SCALDING OIL INTO THE POTS WHERE THE THIEVES WERE LYING IN WAIT.

MORGIANA FILLED EVERY POT WITH SCALDING OIL, KILLING THE MEN WHO MEANT TO DESTROY HER MASTER.

THERE. IT IS DONE, AND THE CAPTAIN'S MEN ARE NO LONGER A THREAT.

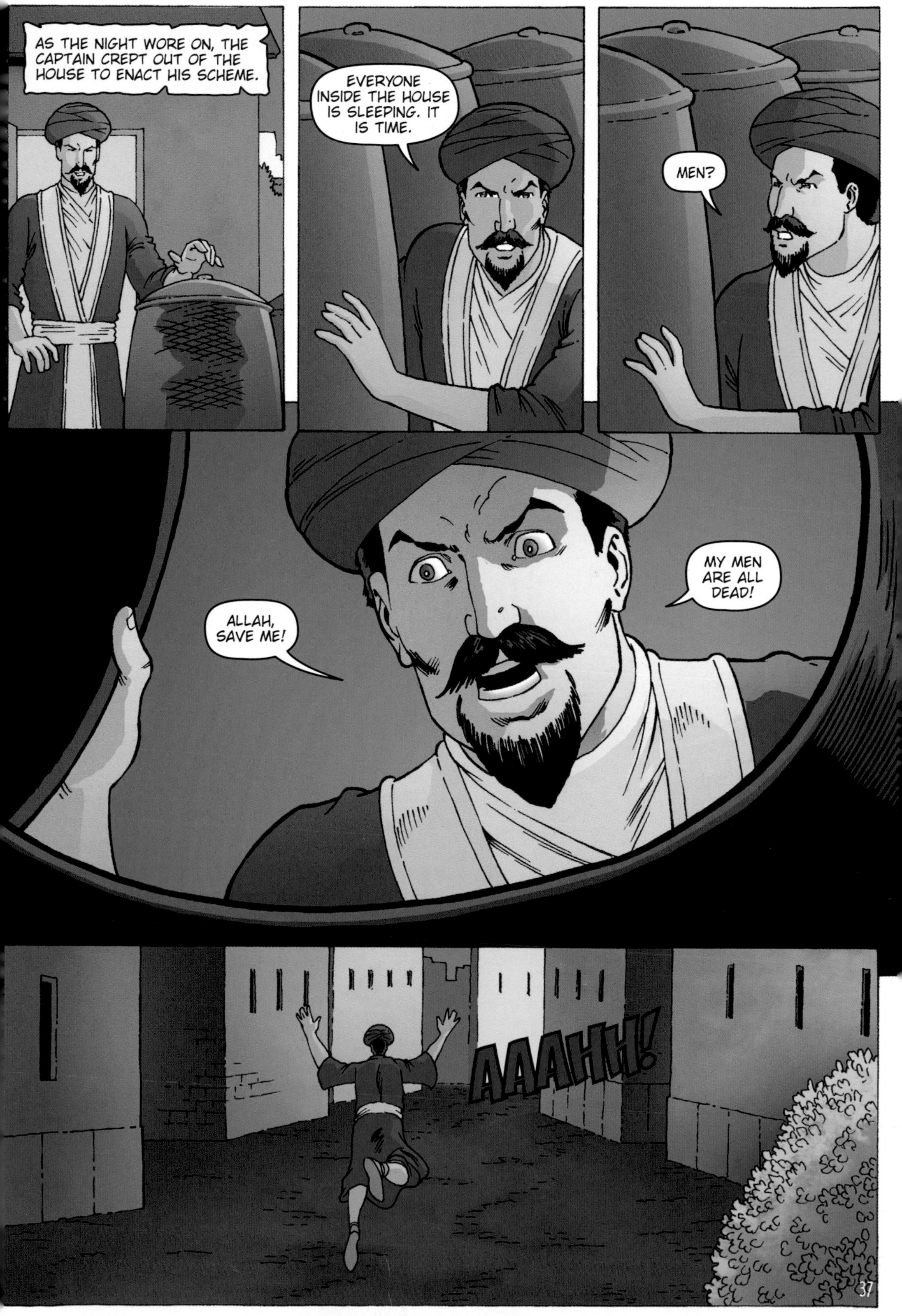
AS THE NIGHT WORE ON, THE CAPTAIN CREPT OUT OF THE HOUSE TO ENACT HIS SCHEME.
EVERYONE INSIDE THE HOUSE IS SLEEPING. IT IS TIME.
MEN?
ALLAH, SAVE ME!
MY MEN ARE ALL DEAD!
AAAHH!

THE NEXT MORNING, ALI BABA WAS SURPRISED TO FIND THAT HIS GUEST WAS GONE.

WHERE IS THE MERCHANT? HIS POTS ARE STILL OUTSIDE, BUT I HAVE NOT SEEN HIM.

I HAVE SOMETHING TO SHOW YOU.

WILL YOU FOLLOW ME?

PLEASE LOOK INSIDE, AND TELL ME WHAT YOU SEE.

AHHHH!

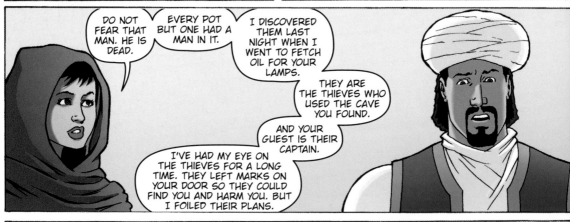

DO NOT FEAR THAT MAN. HE IS DEAD.

EVERY POT BUT ONE HAD A MAN IN IT.

I DISCOVERED THEM LAST NIGHT WHEN I WENT TO FETCH OIL FOR YOUR LAMPS.

THEY ARE THE THIEVES WHO USED THE CAVE YOU FOUND.

AND YOUR GUEST IS THEIR CAPTAIN.

I'VE HAD MY EYE ON THE THIEVES FOR A LONG TIME. THEY LEFT MARKS ON YOUR DOOR SO THEY COULD FIND YOU AND HARM YOU. BUT I FOILED THEIR PLANS.

YOU HAVE SAVED US! HOW CAN I REPAY YOU?

LET US TALK LATER. YOU MUST BURY THESE BODIES WITHOUT DELAY.

38

MORGIANA'S DANCE

*B*ACK AT THE CAVE, THE CAPTAIN WAS FURIOUS.

THIS ... MUST ... END!

I WILL NOT GIVE UP.

I WILL RETURN TO THE VILLAGE AND FIND A WAY TO KILL THE MAN WHO HAS BEEN VISITING MY CAVE.

THE CAPTAIN ONCE AGAIN DISGUISED HIMSELF AS A MERCHANT. THEN HE LEFT TO CARRY OUT HIS NEW SCHEME.

THE CAPTAIN RETURNED TO ALI BABA'S VILLAGE.

HE TALKED TO LOCAL MERCHANTS. HE WAS SURE THEY WOULD HAVE HEARD ABOUT HIS MURDERED MEN. HE THOUGHT PERHAPS ALI BABA HAD BEEN PUNISHED FOR THE CRIME.

GOOD SIR, HAS ANYTHING INTERESTING HAPPENED IN YOUR TOWN LATELY?

NO, KIND MERCHANT. JUST THE USUAL DAILY BUSINESS.

THE MAN WHO CAME TO MY CAVE MUST BE SHREWD INDEED! HE HAS HIDDEN HIS CRIME FROM EVERYONE.

I'D BETTER COME UP WITH A VERY GOOD PLAN.

OTHERWISE, I'LL PERISH AT HIS HANDS.

THE CAPTAIN OPENED A SHOP IN TOWN TO BE CLOSE TO ALI BABA.

THANK YOU FOR RENTING THIS SHOP TO ME.

I BELIEVE THE LOCATION WILL BE MOST PROFITABLE.

A FEW DAYS LATER, KASIM'S SON MET THE CAPTAIN.

GREETINGS, MERCHANT. ARE YOU NEW TO THIS TOWN?

I AM. MY NAME IS KHWAJAH HASAN.

AH, I RUN THE STORE ACROSS THE WAY. IF YOU EVER NEED HELP, JUST ASK ME.

LATER THAT DAY, ALI BABA CAME TO VISIT HIS NEPHEW'S SHOP.

COULD THAT BE THE MAN?

WHO WAS THAT MAN? HE SEEMED QUITE FRIENDLY.

THAT IS MY UNCLE, ALI BABA.

I SEE. THANK YOU, KIND SIR.

FROM THAT DAY FORWARD, THE CAPTAIN WAS ESPECIALLY FRIENDLY TO KASIM'S SON ...

YOU HAVE SHOWN ME MUCH GENEROSITY OF LATE, KHWAJAH HASAN.

LET ME ENTERTAIN YOU AT MY UNCLE'S HOUSE.

I WOULD BE HONORED TO BE YOUR GUEST.

UNCLE, THIS IS KHWAJAH HASAN.

GREETINGS, FRIEND! IT IS AN HONOR.

THE HONOR IS ALL MINE.

ALI BABA ASKED MORGIANA TO TAKE GOOD CARE OF HIS HOUSEGUEST.

PREPARE A FEAST FOR MY NEPHEW'S NEW FRIEND.

DO NOT WORRY. LEAVE EVERYTHING IN MY HANDS.

BUT WHEN ALI BABA INVITED THE CAPTAIN TO DINNER, THE CAPTAIN SAID SOMETHING SURPRISING.

FRIEND, ARE YOU READY TO EAT?

SADLY, I CANNOT DINE WITH YOU. MY DOCTOR HAS FORBIDDEN ME TO EAT SALT.

THAT IS NO CONCERN. I WILL TELL MY SERVANTS NOT TO SEASON THE FOOD.

MORGIANA, OUR GUEST REQUIRES THAT THE MEAT BE PREPARED WITHOUT SALT.

SEE THAT IT IS DONE.

I MUST SEE THIS MAN WHO WILL EAT MEAT WITHOUT SALT.

MORGIANA HELPED SERVE THE MEAL SO THAT SHE COULD GET A GOOD LOOK AT THE GUEST.

YOUR DINNER, MY LORDS ...

OUR DINNER GUEST IS THE CAPTAIN OF THE THIEVES! HE HAS A KNIFE. HE MUST INTEND TO DO MY MASTER IN.

MORGIANA WASTED NO TIME IN TELLING ABDULLAH ALL SHE KNEW.

OUR DINNER GUEST IS THE VILLAIN.

HE IS HERE TO HARM OUR MASTER.

WE MUST STOP THE EVIL MAN AND END THIS THREAT.

GRAB YOUR TAMBOURINE AND FOLLOW ME.

WE WILL FOIL THE CAPTAIN'S PLAN ONCE AND FOR ALL.

MASTER, MAY WE ENTERTAIN YOU BEFORE DINNER? I WISH TO SHOW YOUR GUEST A VERY SPECIAL DANCE. I WILL PERFORM WHILE HOLDING TWO STEEL BLADES IN MY HANDS!

OF COURSE. THIS DANCE WILL BE A SIGHT INDEED.

TA TA TA TA TA TA TA TA TA TA

MORGIANA DANCED HER WAY OVER TO THE CAPTAIN.

WHEN SHE WAS CLOSE ENOUGH, SHE STABBED HIM IN THE HEART.

MORGIANA, YOU HAVE RUINED ME!

WHAT HAVE YOU DONE?

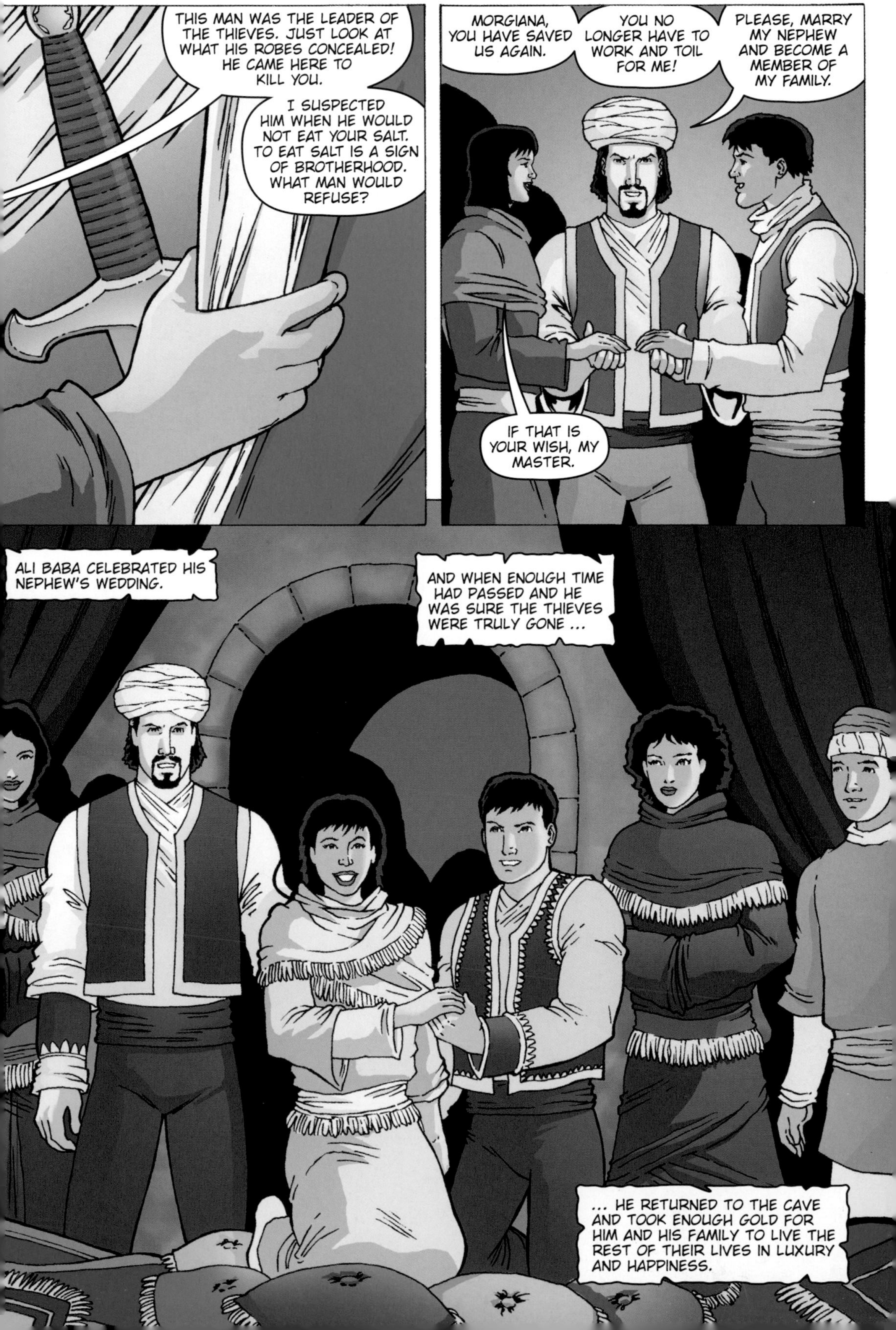
THIS MAN WAS THE LEADER OF THE THIEVES. JUST LOOK AT WHAT HIS ROBES CONCEALED! HE CAME HERE TO KILL YOU.
I SUSPECTED HIM WHEN HE WOULD NOT EAT YOUR SALT. TO EAT SALT IS A SIGN OF BROTHERHOOD. WHAT MAN WOULD REFUSE?
MORGIANA, YOU HAVE SAVED US AGAIN.
YOU NO LONGER HAVE TO WORK AND TOIL FOR ME!
PLEASE, MARRY MY NEPHEW AND BECOME A MEMBER OF MY FAMILY.
IF THAT IS YOUR WISH, MY MASTER.
ALI BABA CELEBRATED HIS NEPHEW'S WEDDING.
AND WHEN ENOUGH TIME HAD PASSED AND HE WAS SURE THE THIEVES WERE TRULY GONE ...
... HE RETURNED TO THE CAVE AND TOOK ENOUGH GOLD FOR HIM AND HIS FAMILY TO LIVE THE REST OF THEIR LIVES IN LUXURY AND HAPPINESS.

GLOSSARY AND PRONUNCIATION GUIDE

ALLAH: the word for God in the Islamic faith

FOIL: to stop or to defeat

MERCHANT: someone who makes money by selling goods

MOURNING: to be very sad for someone who has died

PAUPER (*paw*-puhr): a very poor person

PERSIA: modern-day Iran

ROGUE (*rohg*): a dishonest person

SCIMITAR (*sih*-meh-tahr): a sword with a curved blade

SHROUD: a cloth used to wrap a body for burial

SUET (*soo*-it): animal fat

original pencil sketch from pa

FURTHER READING AND WEBSITES

Croall, Marie P. *Sinbad: Sailing Into Peril*. Minneapolis: Graphic Universe, 2008. Read all about the adventures of Sinbad, another character from the Arabian Nights stories.

Hurwitz, Johanna. *The Adventures of Ali Baba Bernstein*. New York: Morrow, 1985. When David Bernstein decides to change his name to Ali Baba, all kinds of strange and exciting things begin to happen.

Smith, Philip. *Aladdin and Other Favorite Arabian Nights Stories*. New York: Dover, 1993. This book contains six Arabian Nights tales, including *Ali Baba and the Forty Thieves*.

Ali Baba and the Forty Thieves
http://www.pitt.edu/~dash/alibaba.html
At this website, you can read the story of Ali Baba online.

Global Connections: The Middle East
http://www.pbs.org/wgbh/globalconnections/mideast/index.html
This site features detailed information on the Middle East—the region of the world where the Arabian Nights tales began.

CREATING *ALI BABA: FOOLING THE FORTY THIEVES*

To create the story of *Ali Baba*, author Marie P. Croall relied heavily on *Arabian Nights Volume I: The Marvels and Wonders of the Thousand and One Nights*, adapted from Richard F. Burton's unexpurgated translation by Jack Zipes. Artist Clint Hilinski referred to multiple historical resources and worked closely with art historian Allan T. Kohl to make the story's rich imagery come alive.

INDEX

Abdullah, 34–35, 43–45

Ali Baba: encountering the thieves, 7–11; exploring the cave, 12–13; meeting the captain of the thieves, 34

Ali Baba's wife, 6, 14–18, 26–27

Baba Mustafa, 29–32

captain of the thieves, 9–12, 21–22, 31–45

cave, 10–13, 20–22, 24–26, 31, 33, 45

forty thieves, 7–11, 21–22, 31, 33–38

gold, 9–10, 12–16, 18–20, 26, 31, 45

Kasim, 6, 18–30

Kasim's son, 40–42, 45

Kasim's wife, 6, 17–19, 23–25, 27

Morgiana, 27–30, 32–36, 38, 42–45

Persia, 6, 20

pharmacist, 28

ABOUT THE AUTHOR AND THE ARTIST

MARIE P. CROALL lives in Cary, North Carolina, with her loving husband and four wonderful cats. She has written for Marvel, DC, Moonstone Books, Devil's Due, and Harris Comics. She has also completed a self-published graphic novel and a short film. Croall has spent much of her life reading fables and legends from the Middle East and Asia and enjoys discovering new things about different cultures.

CLINT HILINSKI grew up in Esko, Minnesota, where he became interested in art at an early age. He continued studying art at the University of Wisconsin, Superior, where he received his bachelor's degree in fine art. Hilinski's influences include Jim Lee, Alan Davis, and Adam Hughes. He has worked as an illustrator for DC, Image, Dark Horse, and many other companies. Hilinski has worked on titles such as *Sinbad, Justice League of America, Xena, Voltron,* and *GI Joe.*